The Prestige
Nottingha

C000070944

John Banks
With additional input from F P Groves

Photography by G H F Atkins
With additional material from the Senior Transport Archive

Front cover: Trams, trolleybuses and motorbuses running alongside one another were a feature of the Nottingham scene from 1927, when trolleybuses were introduced, to 1936, when the last tram ran. *(G S Cooper)*

Back cover: In 1937 the Nottingham fleet became 100% AEC. The Regent double-decker epitomised the fleet for more than 40 years. The first appeared in 1930 and the last was withdrawn in 1976. Number **108** (**TV 4941**) was a 1931 example, fitted with Park Royal bodywork, which was photographed in August 1934. *(GHFA)*

Title page: The bus stop for motor and trolleybus services to Trent Bridge in a quiet winter's evening Old Market Square scene. Number **180** (**BTO 24**) from Mapperley was waiting to depart for Trent Bridge. Number 180 was an AEC Regent of 1936 which had bodywork by Metro-Cammell. Night photography was a Geoffrey Atkins speciality: this one was taken in February 1937. *(GHFA)*

Below: In this scene at Trent Bridge depot one of the earliest Nottingham trolleybuses, No. **9** (**TO 5010**), a Short Bros-bodied Railless of 1927, was standing alongside a quartet of tramcars. Numbers **117**, **125**, **111** and **118** dated from 1907/8 and had all been rebuilt with new lower decks and platform vestibules during the 1920s. All were awaiting withdrawal. *(GHFA)*

>> *Opposite page:* Geoffrey Atkins was no fair-weather photographer: not for him mothballing the cameras during the winter months. In this February 1934 view in Mansfield Road he tackled misty conditions and produced a fine portrait of trolleybus No. **21** (**TV 751**), a 1930 English Electric 60-seat six-wheeler in the later livery. *(GHFA)*

*Mapperley, on the hill to Nottingham, circa 1911. Tramcar No. **120** of 1908 displays its original specification open vestibules. (GHFA Collection)*

INTRODUCTION

There is nobody better qualified to illustrate this volume and its forthcoming companion covering the municipally operated trams, trolleybuses and buses in Nottingham than Geoffrey Atkins, who was born in that city in 1912. Geoffrey took his first photograph of a Nottingham vehicle in 1927 and his most recent dates from 2001. Thus there is dedicated, comprehensive coverage of some three-quarters of a century of the history of one of the most characterful municipal fleets in the country.

Nottingham City Transport Limited, as it is known in 2002, has its origins in the Nottingham and District Tramways Company Limited, which in 1877 applied to the Board of Trade to construct and operate tramways in Nottingham and suburbs. The Nottingham and District Tramways Order of 1877 authorised the company to operate the tramways worked by animal power in Nottingham and the suburbs of Lenton, Basford and Radford.

Several horse-bus services were already operating in the town; these were not part of the Nottingham and District Tramways Company Limited, although the latter did commence and continue running horse buses, mainly as feeders to the trams, for the whole of its existence.

The first two horse-tram routes commenced on 17th September 1878 from St Peter's Church, a few hundred yards south of the town centre, the Market Place, to Trent Bridge via Carrington Street and Arkwright Street and to London Road via Carrington Street and Station Street and connected the town centre with the two main railway stations, those of the Midland in Station Street and the Great Northern in London Road. Eleven months later, in August 1879, a third route was opened between the Market Place and Carrington in Mansfield Road. In June 1881, a fourth route was inaugurated between the Market Place and Basford Gas Works with a horse-bus connecting service between Basford and Bulwell. In September 1881, a short length of track was laid in Forest Road linking the Basford and Carrington services.

In 1897, Nottingham Corporation took over the tramways and the Nottingham Improvements Act of that year gave authority to use mechanical traction. The horse buses and services were taken over by private operators. Under the Nottingham Corporation Act of 1899, the Corporation had powers to construct and operate electric tramways and construction was started. The first route was between the Market Place and Sherwood, where the first electric-tram depot had been built, and this opened on 1st January 1901. During 1901, a large depot was built at Trent Bridge with accommodation for 80 trams (this building still exists and forms the main works for the city's bus fleet). On 23rd July 1901, a new electric-tram service was inaugurated between the Market Place and Bulwell replacing the horse trams to and from Basford whilst, on 15th October 1901, the Trent Bridge and Station lines were inspected and opened for traffic, with trams on the Station Street route running through to Sherwood, the first cross-town service. Five further routes were opened during 1902 and by the end of that

Nottingham's Wheeler Gate leads south from the Old Market Square. It carried all tram and trolleybus, and motorbus up to 1973, services to and from Trent Bridge via Arkwright Street, West Bridgford, Wilford Bridge and west along Castle Boulevard. In this view, taken circa 1929, one of the trams rebuilt in the 1920s is seen approaching the Old Market Square. The goods delivery traffic still includes some horse-drawn vehicles: the two-wheeled cart emerging from Hounds Gate appears to be without human attendant. (GHFA)

year there were 105 electric trams in service and all the horse trams had been eliminated. More new routes opened to Colwick and London Road in 1907, to Carlton Road in 1910 and the Sherwood route was extended to Arnold in 1915, by which time the fleet had grown to 155 trams. Motorbuses had been tried in 1906, when three Thornycroft double-deckers were obtained for a Carlton Road service, but they were unreliable mechanically and in June 1908 they were replaced by a horse bus service provided by a private operator using Corporation conductors to take the fares.

Top covering of the open-top trams was begun in 1904 and the first covered-top cars delivered new came in 1907; by 1909 72 of the 125-strong fleet had been so fitted.

After the end of the war in 1918, 25 new covered-top trams were ordered and the first of these was delivered in May 1920. At the same time, three new Dennis 35/40 hp single-deck buses were delivered and these inaugurated a service to Bagthorpe in 1920. From those small beginnings the motor bus fleet began to grow

with twelve further Dennis single-deckers being introduced in 1922 and 1923. As a result of an agreement reached in 1924 with Barton of Chilwell, that operator withdrew from the Nottingham-Beeston service and the Corporation purchased 10 buses from Barton (Nottingham fleet numbers 16-25). By July 1928, buses up to fleet number 76 were in use, though some ex-Barton vehicles had been withdrawn.

On 10th April 1927, Nottingham Corporation introduced its first trolleybus service between the Market Place at King Street/Queen Street and Nottingham Road at its junction with Vernon Road. This was started following a visit to Birmingham in January 1924 to inspect the trolleybus system there which had opened in November 1922. The first ten vehicles were built by Railless with Short Bros 52-seat open-staircase bodies, numbered 1-10; No. 10 had been exhibited at the Olympia Exhibition in 1925 and was slightly different from 1-9. This service replaced the trams on the Nottingham Road route. The trolleybuses were an immediate success and more vehicles were required. Railless refused to quote prices or delivery dates but it was possible to place an order with Ransomes, Sims and Jeffries, of Ipswich, for two new vehicles. This pair of trolleybuses were very similar to the ten Railless vehicles but had pneumatic tyres instead of the solid tyres specified for the Railless type. A contemporary observer said that the Railless trolleybuses had dials in the cabs which told a driver exactly where the bus was in relation to the overhead. Drivers tended to position their vehicles in much the same position in line with the overhead, causing the solid tyres to imprint a track in the road surface.

On 1st January 1929, Mr W G Marks, from Chesterfield, was appointed General Manager at Nottingham; there followed a long period of development and expansion and the name of the undertaking was changed to "Nottingham Corporation Passenger Transport Department". Fairly early in 1929, some experiments were tried with various makes of double-deck bus. These were one each from Leyland, AEC, Maudslay, Thornycroft and Sunbeam, this last being a six-wheeler. In consequence an order was placed for 20 AEC Regent double-deckers with English Electric bodies, five of which had centre entrances; delivery started towards the end of 1929.

Earlier, to meet additional requirements and to put maintenance on an organised footing, 20 AEC Reliance single-deck motorbuses were hired from AEC and were later purchased outright. They had Middlesex County Council registrations and a very early version of the 6-type AEC 6-cylinder petrol engine later developed for the AEC Regent. A six-wheeled pneumatic-tyred trolleybus with a Guy chassis was hired from Wolverhampton Corporation for trials and was followed later by a similar but newer Karrier trolleybus from Doncaster Corporation.

There were visits to inspect the trolleybus systems at Doncaster, Wolverhampton and Maidstone before new vehicles were ordered for the Wilford Road to Wells Road conversion, which would replace a single-track tramway with trolleybuses. Twelve vehicles were ordered, six each from English Electric and Ransomes, Sims and Jeffries, which in each case resembled vehicles supplied to Maidstone. The new trolleybus service commenced in February 1930. In the meantime, 40 AEC Regent double-deck motorbuses were delivered during 1930; 20 further examples had been ordered earlier in 1930. Four experimental trolleybuses were hired for trials in 1930. Number 25 was a Guy six-wheeler with a Guy 59 seater body; No. 26 was the first AEC 663T six-wheeled trolleybus to be built, it had bodywork by English Electric; No. 27 was a Karrier E6 with Park Royal 60-seat rear-entrance bodywork and No. 28 was a Thornycroft six-wheeled chassis with a Brush body. Numbers 25 and 26 were returned to their makers at the end of the trials; the chassis of No. 28 was returned to Brush, but the body was retained; No. 27 was retained and purchased, later becoming No. 50 in the fleet. The body of No. 28 was mounted onto a new Karrier chassis in 1933 and became fleet number 1.

The next tram to trolleybus conversion dealt with the Carlton to Wollaton Park route, which included a loop - both ways - via Ilkeston Road, and Western Boulevard, Derby Road (up to Wollaton Park Gates on Derby Road never having been served by trams) - for which 25 new vehicles were obtained. Numbers 25-36 (TV 4463-74) were Karrier E6s with Park Royal 60-seat bodies, whilst Nos 37-49 (TV 4475-87) were Ransomes six-wheelers bodied by Brush also as 60-seaters. At the same time 30 more AEC Regent petrol-engined motorbuses were ordered; 20 had Park Royal 52-seat bodies (Nos 97-116) and Brush Coachworks supplied the bodywork for the ten with fleet numbers 117-26. These were also 52-seaters and had normal elliptical roofs.

The Regents 97-126 were not to be the final petrol-engined buses delivered to Nottingham as in July and August 1932 eight further Park Royal-bodied AEC Regent 52-seaters were delivered. These had chassis with the longer 16ft 3ins wheelbase permitted under the then new Construction and Use Regulations and the bodies featured a distinct rake at the front. They carried fleet numbers 41/2/5-50. Number 48 was converted in 1933 to a normal-control tower wagon and was replaced by a new Regent petrol-engined chassis, registered TV 9435, which became fleet number 48 and was fitted with the body from the original No. 48.

Notts & Derby Traction, who had run trams between Ripley and Nottingham since 1914, withdrew the service in September 1932 so that the erection of trolleybus wiring could be carried out and in July 1933 the Ministry of Transport inspected the Nottingham Corporation section between Cinderhill (the boundary with the Notts & Derby route) and the junction with the Nottingham Road route at

Valley Road. Through-running by Notts & Derby commenced in October 1933 in time for the annual Goose Fair which started on 5th October. Thus Notts & Derby trolleybuses entered and left Nottingham, King Street/Queen Street, via Mansfield Road and Nottingham Road, instead of via Hyson Green - the route the trams had followed.

Because of the financial crisis in 1933, at the height of the Depression, there were few developments that year. In February it was decided to go ahead at the earliest opportunity with the conversion of the Bulwell tram route to trolleybuses and to extend the route to Bulwell Hall Estate. The Colwick Road and Trent Bridge routes were also included in the scheme. Tenders having been invited for the 56 trolleybuses required for this conversion, orders were placed in July 1933 for 35 Karrier and 21 Ransomes six-wheeled chassis. All the Ransomes and 25 of the Karriers were to have Brush coachbuilt bodies and the other 10 Karriers were fitted with Metropolitan-Cammell all-metal bodies.

The new vehicles were delivered between February and June 1934 and the fleet numbers were 51-60 (Karrier E6 chassis bodied by MCCW); 61-85 (Karrier E6 bodied by Brush); 86-106 (Ransomes chassis with bodies by Brush). All the bodies seated 64. There were thus 106 vehicles in the trolleybus fleet, which made it then the largest in the country, and the tramcar fleet was reduced from 127 to 83.

This conversion removed all trams from the west of the City as the Lenton and Radford circular service, which it had been intended to convert to trolleybuses in advance of the Bulwell route, was turned over to motorbuses at the same time (May 1934). This change reflected the views of the new General Manager, J L Gunn, who came from Aberdeen and had succeeded W G Marks early in 1934.

The first oil-engined buses were placed in service in May 1934, these being five AEC Regents with A165 8.8-litre engines and manual gearboxes. They were numbered 127-31 and had Metro-Cammell 54-seat bodies of the style that was to become so widespread during the 1934-40 period, and to a limited extent up to the mid 1950s, but modified with more slender corner upper-deck pillars to suit Nottingham's requirements. These first AEC diesel-engined buses heralded a type which, with progressive developements, became very familiar in Nottingham until the last examples were withdrawn in the 1970s.

Route renumberings are nothing new in Nottingham: the Gallic-influenced upheaval taking place as these words are written had a counterpart in 1933. (GHFA Collection)

The conversion of the Colwick Road route from trams to trolleybuses took place in June 1935 and the route was linked with Bulwell. Thirty new Leyland TTB3 six-wheeled trolleybuses with Metro-Cammell 64-seat all-metal bodies, similar to those on the 1934 Karriers 51-60, were placed in service in June and July 1935; they were numbered 107-36 and they allowed the last of the original ten trolleybuses of 1927 to be withdrawn.

January 1935 saw the delivery of ten more oil-engined AEC Regents with A165 8.8-litre engines and manual gearboxes, 132-41, which had Northern Counties 50-seat bodies; 25 further virtually identical buses, 142-66, followed in July to October 1935. A noteworthy feature - though not uncommon on oil-engined double-deckers of the era - of these Northern Counties bodies was that the upper deck had fewer seats than the lower saloon: 24 against 26.

On 2nd February 1936, the Mapperley tram route was converted to motorbus operation, leaving only the Arnold route still operated by trams. There were 17 replacement buses: further AEC Regents with A165 8.8-litre oil engines, and Metro-Cammell 52-seat bodies (167-83). These were converted to 56-seaters early in their lives following the relaxation of the weight restrictions imposed by the Construction and Use Regulations.

The name of the undertaking was changed to "Nottingham City Transport" in 1936 and in September, the final tram route, to Arnold, was converted to motorbus operation. New AEC Regents were Nos 184-201, which had 7.7-litre A171 engines and manual gearboxes (184-95) or preselector fluid-flywheel transmission (196-201) and Metro-Cammell 54-seat bodies; and Nos 202-13 which were virtually identical to 196-201. These 30 buses were all delivered in August and September of 1936, though Nos 202-13 entered service in October.

With the trams gone, attention was turned in 1937 to replacement of old buses and the development of bus services to growing areas of the city. Forty-five AEC Regents with Cravens 52-seat bodies and five AEC Regal 32-seaters, also bodied by Cravens, were delivered between August 1937 and February 1938; all had AEC 7.7 oil engines and preselector fluid-flywheel transmission and ten of the Regents were fitted with the new A173 version of the engine, which was of the direct injection type. The Regents were numbered 214-58 and the Regals 72-6.

One of the Regents, No. 248, was exhibited at the 1937 Commercial Motor Show at Olympia and had some additional fittings such as interior mirrors, stainless steel handrails and streamlined mouldings (these being the same as on five bodies on AEC Regents which Cravens had supplied to Rochdale Corporation in July 1937). Number 248 also had an upper-deck seat-counting device that showed the word "FULL" when all seats were occupied. The delivery of these 50 AECs allowed the withdrawal of the remaining Dennis buses and thus the fleet became 100% AEC.

1938 and 1939 saw the arrival of the final prewar AEC Regents, which all had A173 direct-injection engines and preselector fluid-flywheel transmission. There were 46 of them, fitted with Metro-Cammell 54-seat bodies, which recommended the fleet-numbering

system as Nos 1-36, plus Nos 51-60. Like all the oil-engined Regents, particularly those with Metro-Cammell bodies, they were sturdy and functional vehicles which served Nottingham reliably for many years.

No further buses or trolleybuses were delivered until 1942, and *Nottingham 2* will look at those wartime vehicles as well as the postwar fleet. However, some second-hand trolleybuses were bought from Southend and Cleethorpes in 1940 (the Cleethorpes vehicles dated from 1937/8 and were newer than any indigenous Nottingham trolleybuses), and from Daimler (an ex-demonstrator) and the Hastings Tramway Company in 1941. The Daimler was also very modern: a 1938 vehicle, it had a Weymann body which had been built to the outline, with interior trim, external beading, destination indicators, etc., then favoured by Hull Corporation in the hope that Daimler would attract orders from that municipality; as it transpired, a forlorn hope. The Southend and Hastings machines were somewhat vintage, dating respectively from 1930 and 1928/9.

Nearly all the photographs used in this book were taken by Geoffrey Atkins *(GHFA)*, and writer and publisher must once again express their profound appreciation of Geoffrey's courtesy in so willingly making his work available; a handful of illustrations from the Senior Transport Archive *(STA)* have filled some gaps: grateful thanks to John Senior for allowing their use.

The captions have benefited from details drawn from Ron Maybray's remarkable written archive; the book *Nottingham City Transport* by F P Groves, published in 1978 by the Transport Publishing Company, has proved useful in preparing the captions, as have the publications of The PSV Circle and The Omnibus Society. Grateful thanks to John Gillham for supplying the maps of Nottingham's tramway and motor/trolleybus systems; to Roy Marshall, another son of Nottingham, for reading the proofs and making numerous suggestions for its improvement; to David and Mary Shaw, indefatigable proofreaders. Finally, the book would have been very much the poorer without the guiding hand of Philip Groves, a former General Manager of Nottingham City Transport, who has contributed much to the text of both Introduction and captions.

John Banks
Romiley, Cheshire.
January 2002

Above: Tramcar No. **20** of 1901 is seen in November 1932 as rebuilt with the new lower saloon by UEC, fitted in 1914, and platform vestibules fitted by Henry Street in the 1920s. The photograph was taken in Mansfield Road and the tram was on service 6 between Jellico Road (Sherwood) and the Radford Circle. *(GHFA)*

Below: Theatre Square in about 1935 was host to rebuilt 1902 car No. **99** on its way to Bulwell on service D (very soon to be converted to trolleybus operation). The new lower saloon and added vestibules are not obscured by the ladies nonchalantly crossing the road in a manner that would see them run over these days. *(GHFA)*

<< *Opposite page:* The Old Market Square seen in May 1932 from the steps of the then quite new Council House. All three trams date from 1914 or later, being of the four-window variety. Only one fleet number is visible, on car No. **167** of 1920 working to Daybrook on service 1. *(GHFA)*

Above: Tramcar No. **142** of 1914 is shown on the steepest section of Woodborough Road on service B to Mapperley in August 1934. The Mapperley route had the steepest gradient on the system and trams used on it were fitted with track brakes. *(GHFA Collection)*

Below: In the final year of the trams, 1927 car No. **182** was working to Arnold on service K, the last tram route to survive. In the background, outside Victoria railway station, is a Nottingham AEC Regent on the Mapperley service, converted in February 1936, and a Notts & Derby trolleybus. *(GHFA)*

Tramcar No. **181** outside the Central Market in King Edward Street at the junction with Lower Parliament Street in March 1934. AEC Reliance motor bus No. **95** (**MY 840**) was on the 26, being followed by a Ransomes trolleybus, only one of which, No. 90 (TV 9347), had entered service by the date of this picture. It could have been on test or driving instruction duty. Another tram of the 181-200 batch is visible behind. The young cyclist looking to his right might just miss the sprightly lady pedestrian. (*GHFA*)

Above: Tramcar No. **195** of 1927, built by English Electric with Peckham bogies, was photographed in Vernon Road in March 1934 heading for Trent Bridge from Bulwell, not long before the route was converted to trolleybus operation. The trolleybus overhead, plainly visible, was known as the "Nottingham catenary suspension system". *(GHFA)*

Below: This is a superb evocation of the last summer of tramcar operation in Nottingham. Old Market Square in September 1936, in bright sunlight following a rain shower, had tramcar No. **196**, also of 1927, on service K to Arnold. The AEC Regent was on service 31 bound for Mapperley, which had been the most recent tram to bus conversion, the preceding February. Another AEC Regent, No. **103** (**TV 4494**) of 1931, can be glimpsed in the background. It was working service 10. *(GHFA)*

Above: In August 1926, Nottingham purchased six Dennis D double-deckers fitted with Short Brothers, of Rochester, bodywork. They were numbered 36-41 (TO 4006-11) and were similar to six Dennis 40/50hp double-deckers which had been acquired in August 1925. The 1925 batch was withdrawn in 1930 and the 1926 examples lasted into 1932. In this photograph a brand new example, unfortunately unidentifiable, gleams for the camera. General Manager John Aldworth's name is prominent on the side panels. The livery is the original maroon and cream, later suppressed on buses, but retained to the end for tramcars. *(STA)*

Below: Dennis 40/50hp double-decker No. **32** (**TO 1897**) stands in Upper Parliament Street circa 1927 whilst working the Hucknall service. *(GHFA Collection)*

Above: Fleet number **34** (**TO 1942**), seen here at Canning Circus circa 1927, was one of the Short Brothers-bodied Dennis 40/50hp buses bought in 1925. The open staircase body had seats for 50. *(GHFA Collection)*

Below: A total of 31 single-deckers on Dennis 35/40hp chassis entered the Nottingham fleet from May 1920 to January 1926 carrying a variety of bodywork from Christopher Dodson, of Willesden, Dennis Brothers, of Guildford, Henry Street, of Nottingham, and Hickman. In another picture of an unidentified bus the body is one of those built by the chassis manufacturer, Dennis. The vehicle is possible one of Nos 7-9 (AU 5890-2) of April 1922. *(STA)*

Above: The chassis specification moved from the 35/40hp chassis to the more powerful 40/50hp version for Dennis single-deckers later in 1926 and in 1927. This example, No. **49** (**TO 6096**), seen in Trinity Square in July 1932, was a 1927 example. The 26-seat front-entrance bodywork, for one-man operation, was built by the Nottingham coachbuilder Henry Street & Company. The vehicle was renumbered 103 in 1932 and withdrawn later that year. *(GHFA)*

Below: Fleet number **43** (**TO 4013**) was a 40/50hp Dennis dating from the previous year, 1926. It also had bodywork by Henry Street, this time to rear-entrance configuration with 29 seats. It was photographed at the Embankment when brand new. *(GHFA Collection)*

Above: This Nottingham Dennis, which is unidentified and about which little is known, is quoted by the photographer from contemporary observation as rebodied by Challands-Ross. It was possibly a Dennis chassis bought to be fitted with a body removed from an ex-Barton chassis and rebodied as shown circa 1927. It was photographed, showing signs of collision damage, outside the City Hospital in April 1929. *(GHFA)*

Below: In 1928 Nottingham turned to the Dennis E when that improved model was available in replacement of the 40/50hp model. Dennis fell out of favour upon the arrival of W G Marks as General Manager in 1929 and no more Dennises were bought thereafter. Nineteen twenty-eight also saw an experiment with the Maudslay *marque*, when five ML4Bs with Vickers 26-seat front-entrance bodies for one-man operation were tried. Number **53** (**TO 7233**) was at Parliament Street depot in August 1933. It was withdrawn the following year. The fitting on the scuttle is believed to have been for carrying a Post Office letterbox. *(GHFA)*

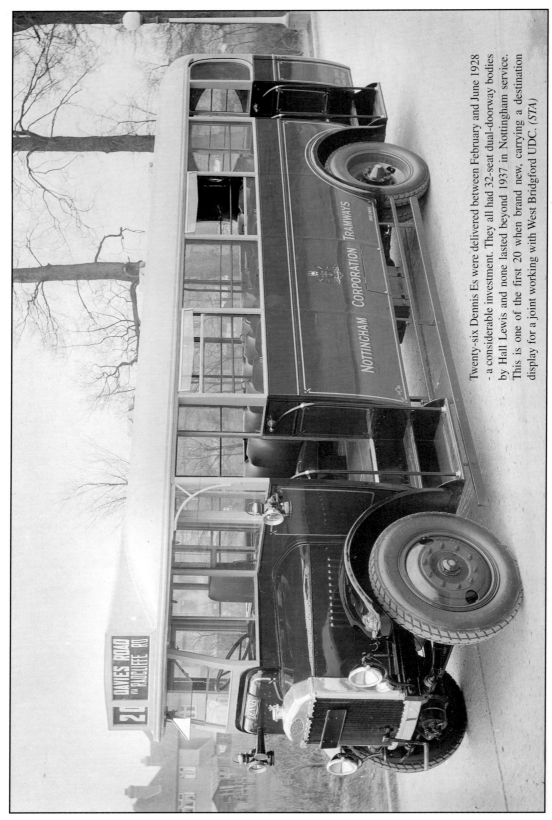

Twenty-six Dennis Es were delivered between February and June 1928 – a considerable investment. They all had 32-seat dual-doorway bodies by Hall Lewis and none lasted beyond 1937 in Nottingham service. This is one of the first 20 when brand new, carrying a destination display for a joint working with West Bridgford UDC. (STA)

Above: In this view of the first Nottingham Dennis E, No. **16** (**TO 7226**), the vehicle can be seen to be fitted with the archaic feature - even in 1929 - of oil side-lamps. The photograph was taken in August of that year in Upper Parliament Street, opposite Barton's private terminus, and the vehicle was working to Bulwell on service 7. *(GHFA)*

Below: Dennis E No. **66** (**TO 7246**) was withdrawn in 1935 after seven years in Nottingham service and was sold to a travelling fairground showman, W Burrows, of Nottingham. Here it is three years later, at the celebrated Nottingham Goose Fair in October 1938, still in Nottingham livery with fleet number, coat of arms and route-number blind. *(GHFA)*

Above: A splendidly varied scene in Mansfield Road in May 1936 includes a rare rear view of a Dennis E, No. **69** (**TO 7249**), on the move in service. Also visible are two Nottingham trolleybuses dating from 1931 (approaching the camera) and 1934, a 1927 tramcar coming from Arnold and a Notts & Derby half-cab trolleybus. The Nottingham system's widely spaced trolleybus wires are very evident: they were later brought closer together. The three-wheeled delivery van with single front motorcycle-type wheel, popularised by such manufacturers as Raleigh, of Nottingham, Reliant and James, was typical of the era. *(GHFA)*

Below: A wet-weather August 1929 view at Gregory Boulevard of the previous year's Dennis E No. **71** (**TO 8171**) in its original livery, working service 2 to Bagthorpe. *(GHFA)*

>> *Opposite page:* Dennis E No. **74** (**TO 8174**) in the later green and cream livery in Stanhope Street in May 1933. Part of Stanhope Street was covered over in later years to become part of Lower Parliament Street garage. *(GHFA)*

On 1st March 1931 Nottingham Corporation took over five Gilfords from Reynolds Bros Bus Service, of Bulwell. The Trent Motor Traction Company Limited acquired the rest of the Reynolds fleet at the same time. NCT had already gained running powers on the Nottingham to Hucknall service, making this the joint purchase of a competitor. The Gilfords were never repainted and were withdrawn later in 1931. Number **105 (RR 9136)**, a 1928 1660T shows the hardly elegant temporary paper fleetname. *(STA)*

Trolleybuses were introduced onto the streets of Nottingham in April 1927 on a route that ran between Nottingham Road, and King Street in the City Centre, for which ten solid-tyred vehicles were bought from Railless; they had Short Brothers 52-seat open-staircase bodywork and two English Electric 35hp motors. The Railless concern was a subsidiary of Short Brothers. These vehicles were among the very first to have four-wheel brakes: a cumbersome system - not power-operated - that involved pushing on the right-hand pedal and simultaneously pulling on a long lever, also on the right. All ten were withdrawn between 1932 and 1935 and sold for scrap, though some are thought to have had a further life as caravans in Derbyshire. Number **2** (**TO 5003**) was at a stop in Sherwood Rise in February 1933 *(above)* and No. **4** (**TO 5005**) was at the King Street/Queen Street terminus in June 1930. The former had tram-type wheel trolleys, whilst No. 4 had Wilkinson sliding trolley heads. The livery was light and dark green and cream, with gold lining-out. *(Both: GHFA)*

<< *Opposite page:* Railless No. **6** (**TO 5007**) turning out from Milton Street in March 1933. This view has been enlarged from a small portion of the negative to show close detail of the body design. Note how slender the front wheels are. *Above:* Railless trolleybus No. **10** (**TO 5011**) was built for the 1925 Commercial Motor Show. It differed from the production batch 1 - 9 in having a flush centre-panel at the front of the upper saloon (compare with No. **3** behind). By the time of this February 1934 view in Lower Parliament Street garage, a driver's door had been inserted into the nearside of the cab. *Below:* The two pneumatic-tyred Ransomes D4s of 1928 are represented by No. **12** (**TO 8622**) at the Nottingham Road/Haydn Road terminus of service 37 in September 1933. Ransomes also built the 52-seat bodywork. The photographer has recorded that the front pneumatic tyres were filled with a "sorbo" rubber material to avoid too great a drop in the event of a puncture. *(All: GHFA)*

The AEC Reliances

The Dennis and Maudslay motor-buses were found wanting, upon his arrival in 1929, by the new incumbent in the General Manager's chair, Mr W G Marks, lately of Chesterfield Corporation. He arranged the loan of demonstrators from a variety of manufacturers and, as a short-term measure, the hiring of 20 AEC Reliances from the Southall manufacturer. The Reliance was by no means common in municipal fleets, but they must have given satisfaction, for they were later purchased and served Nottingham well until withdrawal between 1937 and 1950. Bodywork, to twin-doorway, 30-seat specification, was by Short Brothers, of Rochester. In one of Geoffrey Atkins's superb after-dark shots *(above)*, No. **78** (**MY 535**) was in Huntingdon Street bus station, as *(below)* was No. **80** (**MY 537**). *(GHFA)*

The AEC Reliances

Above: The 20 AEC Reliances arrived in July (13) and August 1929. One of the August deliveries was No. **90** (**MY 836**), seen here in Stanhope Street in March 1935. This part of Stanhope Street was later covered over and became part of Nottingham's Parliament Street garage. *(GHFA)*

Below: In another atmospheric night-time view at Huntingdon Street, taken in 1935, Reliances Nos **96** (**MY 839**) - the last of the batch according to the fleet numbers - stands ahead of No. **91** (**MY 837**). The "MY" registration marks were issued by Middlesex County Council - the home county of the Associated Equipment Company - in the range MY 534 - 842, but not in numerical order of the 77 - 96 fleet number group. In the left background of the picture can be seen the Salvation Army Hall; William Booth was a native of Nottingham. *(GHFA)*

AEC Reliance of July 1929 No. **82** (**MY 539**) in July 1936 at Huntingdon Street bus station. It was working on hire to Trent on a busy holiday Saturday on Trent's service to Doncaster. (*GHFA*)

The First AEC Regents

Above: The end of 1929 saw the first of a long line of Nottingham Corporation AEC Regents delivered. AEC's Regent demonstrator MT 2114 had been on hire and had decided Mr Marks to award a contract to Southall. The first batch, which started a new fleet number series as Nos 1 - 20, had English Electric 51-seat rear-entrance (on Nos 1-15) or 50-seat centre-entrance (Nos 16-20) bodywork. Number **2** (**TV 722**) is shown at Arnold in January 1930, carrying the original livery style. *(GHFA)*

Below: An unidentified example of the centre-entrance buses, Nos 16-20 (TV 736-40), is seen in Long Row in September 1931. All 20 English Electric machines had been withdrawn by 1938. These Nottingham centre-entrance vehicles were in service prior to the well-known Roe-bodied example in Grimsby. *(GHFA)*

At Stanhope Street, outside the bus garage, in April 1935 one each of the rear-entrance and centre-entrance English Electric-bodied AEC Regents, Nos **9** (**TV 729**) and **18** (**TV 738**), illustrate the recently introduced revised livery of green with three cream bands *(this page)*. The batch of 20 English Electric machines was withdrawn between August 1937 and January 1938. Many were scrapped but No. 15 survived to be rebodied by Park Royal for the Mayne, of Manchester, fleet later in 1938. The fleet numbers 1-20 were reused on new Regents with Metro-Cammell bodies. Two further batches, each of ten, of Regents came in 1930, bodied by Short Brothers and Park Royal. Number **25** (**TV 1625**) was a Short Brothers-bodied "camel roof" example, seen *(>> opposite page)* alongside 1935's Northern Counties-bodied No. **132** (**ATV 13**) in the entrance to Parliament Street garage in May 1935. The latter carries the twin driving-lamps favoured by NCT until they became illegal in January 1949. The dark nearside headlight on the older Regent is an orange-lensed foglamp *(All: GHFA)*

Above: A typically bold Geoffrey Atkins portrait of another of the Short Brothers-bodied Regents of 1930, taken at Parliament Street garage in February 1935. A March 1930 delivery, No. **27** (**TV 1627**) lasted until 1938 when it was withdrawn and sold, with six others from the 21-40 series, to Whieldon's Green Bus, of Rugeley. The Short Brothers bodywork had 26 seats upstairs and 24 down. *(GHFA)*

>> *Opposite page:* The Short bodywork, with its peculiar hump in the roofline, is seen here carrying the original livery. The bus is No. **28** (**TV 1628**), photographed in August 1933. *(GHFA)*

The Park Royal bodies on Nottingham's fleet numbers 31-40, new in April and May 1930, were the result of an order placed upon Hall, Lewis & Co., Park Royal's predecessors. The photographer, at the time of taking these February 1935 shots of No. **32** (**TV 1632**) outside Parliament Street garage, gained the information that these bodies were to an AEC design and that the "camel-back" roof effect had been intended to give a low-height appearance to the recently launched Regent as a measure of competition for the very popular Leyland Titan. The nearside-rear view is interesting in that it shows the platform and entrance arrangements, as well as the step to the lower-saloon floor level inside the saloon instead of in the rear bulkhead. This was a typical feature of "camel-roof" bodies. Note the triangular stoplight. *(Both: GHFA)*

Nineteen-thirty's trolleybus deliveries were six-wheelers: six Ransomes D6s and six English Electric vehicles, in each case with bodywork by the chassis manufacturer. The six from Ransomes, Sims and Jefferies Ltd were built to a luxurious standard in that concern's Ipswich works. The chassis ran on 36ins by 8ins pneumatic tyres and the rear bogie was to a Thornycroft patent, one of whose features was a third differential in the rear axles, which equalised the drive among all four rear wheels. This meant, in effect, that each wheel could rotate at a different speed according to tyre diameter and other factors. The interiors were finished with mahogany mouldings and panelling with white enamelled ceilings. The Ransomes patent sub-base carried the trolley booms independently of the roof, which left the latter free of stress, especially during dewirements. This was an advanced specification for a 1930 vehicle and all five lasted - just - into the postwar period. In the view above No. **13** (**TV 743**), in original livery, was at Wells Road terminus on the opening day of service 10, 23rd February 1930. The August 1940 view *(below)* is of No. 16, renumbered as **316**, (**TV 746**), with wartime additions to its livery, masked headlamps and "blue" windows, at Gregory Boulevard. *(Both: GHFA)*

How many bus inspectors does it take to guide a trolleybus driver past some minor road works? Much activity attended these vehicles in Lower Parliament Street at the junction with Milton Street in March 1934. The upper picture, which includes a lovely cameo of the conductor leaning out to watch the trolley booms, is of No. **15** (**TV 745**), another of the 1930 Ransomes six-wheelers. The six English Electric machines, of which No. **23** (**TV 753**) is shown below, were built at the manufacturer's Preston factory. Some of this batch lasted into the late 1940s. *(Both: GHFA)*

Above: Two of the 1930 English Electric trolleybuses feature in this June 1930 view at George Street at its junction with Lower Parliament Street. Number **24** (**TV 754**), the last of the batch, is turning into George Street, whilst No. **20** (**TV 750**) was running east down Lower Parliament Street *en route* from Wilford Road into Wells Road. The original livery is in evidence, and No. 20 was unusual in having white beading round the front of the cab. *(GHFA)*

Below: The later livery in an unusual angle on English Electric trolleybus No. **19** (**TV 749**), the first of the batch of six, seen inside Lower Parliament Street garage in September 1935. The ingenious method of mounting the trolley booms, so that no stress was imparted to the roof panels, is well shown. *(GHFA)*

<< Opposite page: Thirty AEC Regents augmented the motor-bus fleet in 1931: 20 bodied by Park Royal and 10 by Brush; all were 52-seaters. The first of them, and also the first from the Park Royal factory, was No. **97** (**TV 4488**), seen here when brand new in June 1931. Note that the body was of *five-bay* construction. *(STA)*

Above: The 20 Park Royal bodies came in two groups of ten. From the second group, No. **112** (**TV 4945**) was photographed in Stanhope Street in August 1933. It had *six-bay* bodywork. The separate groups of ten were respectively all of five-bay and six-bay construction. *(GHFA)*

Below: The Brush version was also six-bay, and had a much smoother roofline. Number **122** (**TV 4955**) was parked in Stanhope Street in March 1935. *(GHFA)*

These two pictures straddle the prewar trolleybus renumbering scheme. Number **326**, formerly 26, (**TV 4464**) is seen *(above)* at Wollaton Park in May 1940, complete with wartime blackout fittings and livery additions. Two batches of six-wheelers - 12 Park Royal-bodied Karrier E6s and 13 Brush-bodied Ransomes D6s - with 60 seats came in 1931; No. 26 was one of the former. Number **39** (**TV 4477**) *(below)* was one of the Brush/Ransomes machines, seen at Wollaton Park Gates in January 1932 in the original livery of cream and two shades of green. An interesting touch in the body, built to the specification of the General Manager, W G Marks, was that local industry was supported for the seats, which were commissioned - upholstered in Nottingham-green leather - from the Lace Web Spring Company, of Sandiacre. *(Both: GHFA)*

Above: Proof, were it needed, that Geoffrey Atkins was far from being an "only-when-the-sun-is-out" photographer, is found in this chilly view of Gregory Boulevard in January 1940. Piled snow to a depth of two or three feet was making the going hazardous for both pedestrians and vehicles. Number **349**, formerly 49 (**TV 4487**), was the last of the Brush-bodied Ransomes D6s of 1931. *(GHFA)*

Below: Number **341** (**TV 4479**), which had been fleet number 41 when new in 1931, was a similar machine. It lasted, along with ten more of the 1931 machines, into 1950 and is seen at Nottingham Road junction with Vernon Road in September 1948. *(GHFA)*

41

Motor-bus Demonstrators

Above: Nottingham made the fullest use of loaned demonstrators. Their visits to the city were often short and the sun didn't often shine on them: literally or figuratively, for neither Maudslay nor Leyland, Daimler nor Crossley, Thornycroft nor Sunbeam, managed to deflect Mr Marks away from his loyalty to the AEC Regent. And, however bad the weather, Geoffrey Atkins, in the knowledge that the visitors' appearance on Nottingham's streets would be fleeting, was on hand to photograph them. **VC 1778** was a Maudslay ML7B with Northern Counties lowbridge bodywork demonstrated, and photographed in Trinity Square, in October 1929. *(GHFA)*

Below: The protoype Leyland "Hybridge" 48-seater, **TE 9855**, was in Nottingham for a few days in February 1930. It was tracked down by the indefatigable photographer in murky lighting conditions in Long Row. *(GHFA)*

Motor-bus Demonstrators

Above: The Leyland Titan on the previous page was sold later in 1930 to Bury Corporation. Daimler CH6 **VC 6779** went a good deal further north when in March 1932 it joined the Dundee Corporation fleet at the end of its demonstrating days. In an even murkier Trinity Square in December 1930 it is seen being evaluated on Nottingham's Arnold service 20. The highbridge body was a 52-seater by Park Royal. *(GHFA)*

Below: In late 1932 a maroon and cream Crossley Condor, with Crossley bodywork, registered **RG 1676** and having had its petrol engine replaced by a compression-ignition unit, appeared for about a fortnight in Nottingham, where it was photographed in Mansfield Road. For once the sun was shining, though not on Crossley's salesman, for none were ordered. This one was later sold to Northampton Corporation. *(GHFA)*

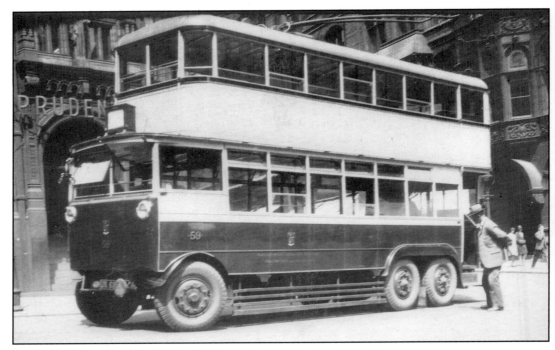

Trolleybus Demonstrators

Above: Wolverhampton Corporation No. **59** (**UK 6359**), a Guy BTX bodied by Christopher Dodson, of Willesden, was on hire to Nottingham for a short period in 1929. It is seen in May of that year at the King Street/Queen Street junction. *(GHFA)*

Below: Another Guy BTX, this time owned and bodied by Guy Motors Limited (as a 59-seater), and registered **UK 8948**, was tried in 1930. It was numbered **25** during its stay in Nottingham. In December 1930, having been sent back from Nottingham, it went from Guy to Pontypridd Urban District Council, who purchased it in April 1931 and gave it the fleet number 8. *(GHFA)*

Trolleybus Demonstrators

Above: Middlesex-registered **HX 1460** was an AEC 663T (the first, according to its chassis number 663T001) with English Electric electrical and auto-acceleration equipment and 60-seat bodywork. It was in Nottingham in October 1930, and was photographed at Wells Road. This vehicle, rebodied and reregistered, later went into the Southend-on-Sea Corporation fleet. *(GHFA)*

Below: Leyland-GEC TTB demonstrator **TJ 939**, built in 1932 and fitted with Leyland's own bodywork, in Upper Parliament Street in May 1933 on the Carlton to Wollaton Park service. It was in Birmingham livery with that operator's fleet number **17**. *(GHFA)*

Trolleybus Demonstrators

Above: Karrier-Clough E6 demonstrator **VH 3305** with Park Royal 60-seater bodywork was on trial in Parliament Street in October 1930. *(GHFA)*

Below: **VH 3305** had run as Nottingham's fleet number 27 during its trials in the city. The vehicle was later purchased by Nottingham and allocated the number **50**. In this view, its appearance much altered by the substitution of a plain panel for the dummy radiator, it was at Gregory Boulevard in May 1933. It was renumbered in 1939 as 350 and was withdrawn in 1948. In later life it was used on trials near Trent Bridge works with one boom with a single trolleyhead suitably insulated for use on wires about twelve inches apart. It was scrapped in 1949 by a Lichfield dealer. *(GHFA)*

Trolleybus Demonstrators

Above: The fourth demonstrator to put in a spell in Nottingham in 1930 was **TV 3460**, a Thornycroft BD with a Brush motor and other electrical equipment by BTH. The body, a 60-seater, was also by Brush. It was brand new in this picture taken at Wells Road, running under fleet number **28**. *(GHFA Collection)*

Below: The chassis of TV 3460 was returned to Brush Coachworks in 1931 but the body was retained and in 1933 was mounted on a new Karrier E6A chassis. Registered **TV 8473**, the new combination was given the fleet number **1**. It was photographed passing west along Upper Parliament Street in Theatre Square on service 39 shortly after entering service in May 1933. It was withdrawn in 1948. *(GHFA)*

<< *Opposite page:* Eight Park Royal-bodied 56-seat, petrol-engined AEC Regents arrived in 1939. They had the then newly authorised longer wheelbase of 16ft 3ins. This one is No. **49** (**TV 6750**) when brand new. In 1947 No. 49 was fitted with a diesel engine. It was withdrawn in 1949.

This page: Number **48** (**TV 6749**) of the same batch *(right)* was withdrawn in 1933 and its

chassis used as the basis for a normal-control tower wagon with the fleet number **4**. It survives today at the East Anglian Transport Museum, Carlton Colville. The body from No. 48 was mounted onto a new AEC Regent chassis, registered **TV 9435** *(above)*, retaining the fleet number **48**, in 1933. That combination lasted in service until February 1949. *(STA [1]; GHFA [3])*

Above: This AEC Regent demonstrator ran in Nottingham, with fleet number **107A** and registration **TV 4867**, from January to April 1932. The chassis was one of the earliest with the 16ft 3ins wheelbase, recently allowed under the then new Construction & Use Regulations. It had a lightweight body, seating 56, built by Park Royal. The bus had been exhibited by AEC at the 1931 Commercial Motor Show. Despite Nottingham's commitment to the AEC *marque*, this bus was not retained. It was acquired by White, of Cardiff, and thence passed into the Western Welsh fleet in 1935. *(GHFA)*

Below: The first oil-engined buses purchased for the Nottingham fleet arrived in May 1934. The batch of five is represented by No. **131** (**AAU 182**), brand new on delivery, at Stanhope Street. *(GHFA)*

This creative night-time shot at the west end of the Old Market Square dates from January 1937. The view shows the Queen Victoria statue, Griffin & Spalding's department store and the Council House, whose clock proclaims the time as 7.50pm. Trolleybus **52** (**TV 9315**) was a Karrier E6 with Metro-Cammell 64-seat metal-framed bodywork, which had been new in May 1934. It survived as No. 352 until March 1952. (*GHFA*)

There were ten of the Metro-Cammell metal-framed trolleybuses on Karrier E6 chassis in 1934, which took the fleet number series 51-60. Two more of them are illustrated here: No. **55** (**TV 9311**) and No. **357**, formerly 57 (**TV 9317**). Number 55 *(above)* features in an interesting picture at Old Market Place in May 1934, with in the background a gantry - one of several - used for raising spoil from below ground during the construction of a trunk sewer. In the lower picture, another from the early months of the Second World War, No. 357 was at Wollaton Park. The stove-like apparatus on the extreme right of the picture was a paraffin smokescreen burner, one of many hundreds scattered around the city boundary designed to frustrate enemy aircrew during bombing raids. *(Both: GHFA)*

In 1934 there were also Brush composite-bodied trolleybuses on both Karrier and Ransomes chassis. The main picture is of Ransomes No. **87 (TV 9344)** in as-built condition before delivery to Nottingham. In the inset can be seen No. **106 (TV 9360)**, another Ransomes, in Nottingham service at Beastmarket Hill in February 1935. It was then eight months old. (*STA; GHFA*)

More Metal-Framed Bodywork

Above: The Corporation were very satisfied with the Metro-Cammell metal-framed bodies on the 1934 Karriers. In 1935, following consultation with Birmingham Corporation about their similar vehicles, 30 Leyland TTBs with similar bodywork were purchased. The first of them, No. **107** (**ATV 170**), and at least five others are seen when new in May 1935 inside Parliament Street depot. In practice, these vehicles were never based at this, the main, depot. *(GHFA)*

Below: An all-too-rare rear view of a prewar trolleybus in service is of No. **109** (**ATV 172**) in a bustling traffic scene at the top of Wheeler Gate in December 1935. The rear bumper on the trolleybus was not unusual in that era; the feature disappeared with the advent of bus washing machines. These Leylands were unusual in having large wheel-hubs on the front wheels, identical to those on the rear. Another of the batch is heading towards the camera, masked by an Armstrong Siddeley and a Ford 8hp Y-type saloon (new for £100). *(GHFA)*

More Oil-Engined AEC Regents

Above: In 1935 twenty-five AEC Regents, with 8.8-litre A165 oil engines (which demanded the protruding radiator), manual gearboxes and Northern Counties metal-framed bodies entered service. The seating arrangement of the 50-seat bodies was unusual in that there were 24 upstairs and 26 down. The last of the batch 142-66, No. **166** (**BAU 824**) was outside Parliament Street garage in June 1936. *(GHFA)*

Below: Number **158** (**BAU 816**) is seen in a postwar, July 1949, view at Long Row having come off service 3 to Radford. Note the revised position of the twin driving lamps following the January 1949 change in regulations, and the later type of roll-down radiator blind. *(GHFA)*

Above: The motorbus fleet was augmented in 1936 by the delivery of no fewer than 47 oil-engined AEC Regent double-deckers with Metro-Cammell metal-framed bodies. They were subdivided into three batches: Nos 167-83 had 8.8-litre A165 engines, manual gearboxes and 52-seat bodies; 184-95 had the smaller 7.7-litre A171 engine, manual gearboxes and 54 seats; 196-213 were also 7.7-litre 54-seaters, but with preselector gearboxes and fluid flywheels. Number **195** (**BTV 582**) is seen at Parliament Street bus depot when new in September 1936. *(GHFA)*

Below: Number **174** (**BTO 18**), in a 1937 view, was at the timing point in the Old Market Square on the way from Mapperley to Trent Bridge. *(GHFA)*

The 1936 AEC Regents in Service

Above: An imposing photograph of the radiator and engine panel of 8.8-litre AEC Regent No. **176** (**BTO 20**) in Long Row in June 1936. The bus had been delivered the previous February. It was withdrawn in 1949 and went on to run for a travelling fairground showman. The picture was taken to illustrate the early type of radiator shutter fitted to oil-engined AEC Regents. *(GHFA)*

Below: At the west end of the Old Market Square, No. **182** (**BTO 26**) waits to depart to Trent Bridge on service 35 from Mapperley, followed by No. **211** (**CTO 385**) which is arriving from Arnold on service 20. These buses were withdrawn respectively in 1949 and 1950. *(GHFA)*

This page: Nineteen-thirty-seven and early 1938 saw the delivery of a further 45 AEC Regents with 7.7-litre engines. These buses took the fleet numbering from 214 to 258. Ten had the AEC A173 direct-injection engine, which was at that time still in the development stage, and the remaining 35 had the earlier A171 type with Ricardo Comet 3 cylinder head. Number **248** (**DAU 490**), bodied - as was the rest of the batch - by Cravens, had additional decorative beading on the body and had been exhibited at the 1937 Commercial Motor Show at Earls Court. Some of the gloss remained in these January 1938 shots in Stanhope Street. *(Both: GHFA)*

>> *Opposite page:* Number **229** (**DAU 471**) of the 1937 batch of Cravens-bodied Regents was painted gold for the Golden Jubilee of Nottingham Corporation's ownership of the undertaking in 1947. There were also five AEC Regals in 1937, with Cravens 32-seat bodies. They had 7.7-litre engines, preselector gearboxes and fluid flywheels. One of them is seen when brand new. *(GHFA; STA)*

The double-deck Cravens bodies were cheaper to buy than the Metro-Cammell units, but had to be rebuilt in the early postwar period, thus costing overall far more than the Metro-Cammell product.

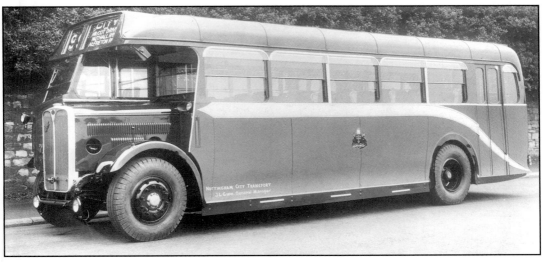

The 1937 AEC Regals

Above: The 1937 AEC Regals were bought to cover the two routes with low bridges: Bulwell Market to Cemetery; and Trent Bridge to Sneinton Dale. **DAU 454** had originally had the fleet number 75; it was renumbered 279 in March 1944 and then again to **779** in June 1948. It is seen in June 1949 at Granby Street in Nottingham. *(GHFA)*

Below: **DAU 454** was renumbered yet again, as **801** in September 1959, at the time of its conversion for use as a mobile staff-canteen. It was at Trent Bridge (Embankment) terminus. It survived in this form until August 1968 when it was sold for scrap. *(GHFA)*

The Final Prewar AEC Regents

Above: In 1938 a batch of 30 AEC Regents was delivered. All had AEC A173 7.7-litre oil engines, preselector gearboxes and fluid flywheel transmissions. The 54-seat bodywork was of metal-framed construction by Metro-Cammell. These vehicles were long-lived in the fleet, and were not withdrawn until 1955-8. In this 1938 photograph, from right to left, can be seen Nos **1**, **2**, **3** and **4** (**ETO 485-8**) prior to delivery from Metro-Cammell. *(STA)*

Below: Sixteen more Regents came in 1939, all but three to the same specification bodily and mechanically as that of the 1938 machines. The odd three had centrifugal clutches instead of fluid flywheels. Number **32** (**FTO 615**) was inside Sherwood garage in April 1955, two years before its withdrawal. *(GHFA)*

Second-Hand Trolleybuses

Above: To ease the shortage of rolling stock in the early part of the Second World War, second-hand trolleybuses were acquired from a number of operators. Numbers 302/3 (JN 60/1) were 1930 English Electric 6-wheelers with 56-seat bodies, which came from Southend-on-Sea Corporation in October 1940. This one is No. **302** (**JN 60**), seen at Trent Bridge in March 1941. Both were withdrawn in 1945. *(GHFA)*

Below: Nottingham was able to acquire six 1928/9 Guy BTX centre-entrance single-deckers with Ransomes 32-seat bodies from Hastings Tramways in November 1941. They took the fleet numbers 304-9 and the first of them, No. **306** (**DY 5120**), was at Wollaton Park in August 1943. Nicknamed "Kiddy Cars", they were usually to be found on the more lightly used Trent Bridge-London Road-City-Derby Road-Wollaton Park service 95. *(GHFA)*

Above: Four AEC 661Ts came from Cleethorpes in October 1940. These Park Royal-bodied 56-seaters were, when they were acquired, the newest trolleybuses in the Nottingham fleet. The fleet numbers were 437-40, and the first of them, No. **437** (**FW 8995**), was photographed at Vernon Road in August 1941. Note the blast-protection tape on the house windows. *(GHFA)*

Below left: From the rear, visibility markings to help other road users in the wartime blackout were restricted to a single white stripe, demonstrated by No. **343** (**TV 4481**), a 1931 Brush-bodied Ransomes. By this time the registration number had to be carried in an illuminated box. *(GHFA)*

Below right: AEC Regent No. **202** (**CTO 376**) of 1936, seen in Turney Street in 1941, shows the immersion-heater in the radiator, which was plugged into the city's power supply. This practice helped keep engines warm during open-air dispersal parking during the war. *(GHFA Collection)*

The Effects of War

Above: The photographer, whilst employed on wartime fire-watching duties in May 1941, took this picture of Long Row in which seven AEC Regents and two trolleybuses, all with blackout white markings, appear. The rectangular objects to the left of the picture were emergency water tanks. The white circle on the road was to warn trolleybus drivers to take their foot off the power pedal to avoid arcing on an overhead insulated section. *(GHFA)*

Below: Nottingham Forest, a large green area about a mile north of the city centre, was host during the war to Corporation buses on dispersal parking: a wise precaution, as one direct hit on a crowded bus garage at night or during a daytime off-peak period could have destroyed scores of buses. Leading this line-up was 1939 AEC Regent No. **32** (**FTO 615**), which had been in use on a trolleybus service. The third in line is No. **202** (**CTO 376**) again. *(GHFA)*

With the illustrations on the previous three pages we have brought our look at the development (and decline, in the case of the trams) of Nottingham's municipal transport systems into the early months of the 1939-45 war. The war years saw a change in the composition of the fleet in that AEC Regents were no longer available (it would be 1949 before the next new Regents) and - *faute de mieux* - Guys and Daimlers were acquired, as were a number of second-hand buses (which included some AECs). The postwar decades saw the AEC Regent re-established, the trolleybus fleet renewed, the familiar move towards rear-engined buses and one-man operation, and - *mirabile dictu* - the planned reintroduction, as the new millennium dawned, of trams. All these aspects of the story will be considered in, *Nottingham 2*. For the moment, then, we leave Nottingham's prewar municipal fleet with a look at a Leyland lorry **TV 842**, which, with the aid of a monstrous Ruston-Bucyrus excavator, was clearing snow in Milton Street in January 1940; and an imposing Leyland-Metz turntable fire-escape **TV 3810**, photographed in the late 1930s. *(Both: GHFA)*

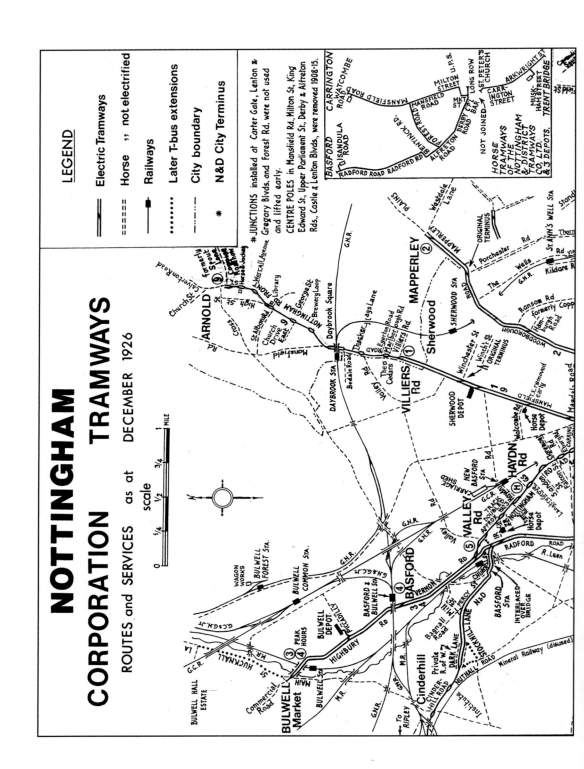

NOTTINGHAM CORPORATION TRAMWAYS

ROUTES and SERVICES   as at   DECEMBER 1926

LEGEND

══════ Electric Tramways

====== Horse ,, not electrified

▬▬▬ Railways

········· Later T-bus extensions

――――― City boundary

✳ N&D City Terminus

#JUNCTIONS installed at Carter Gate, Lenton & Gregory Blvds. and Forest Rd. were not used and lifted early.

CENTRE POLES in Mansfield Rd, Milton St, King Edward St., Upper Parliament St., Derby & Alfreton Rds., Castle & Lenton Blvds., were removed 1908-15.

scale

0   ¼   ½   ¾   1   MILE

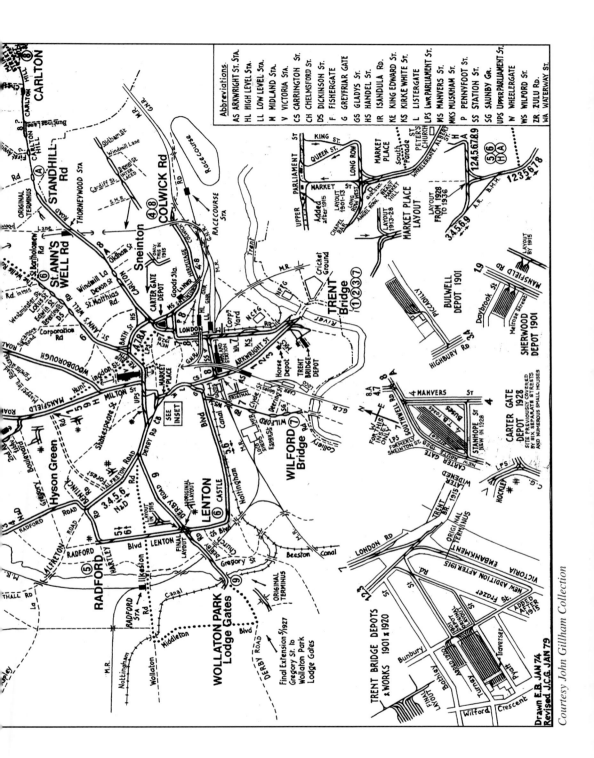

Courtesy John Gillham Collection

Drawn E.B. JAN 74
Revised J.C.G. JAN 79

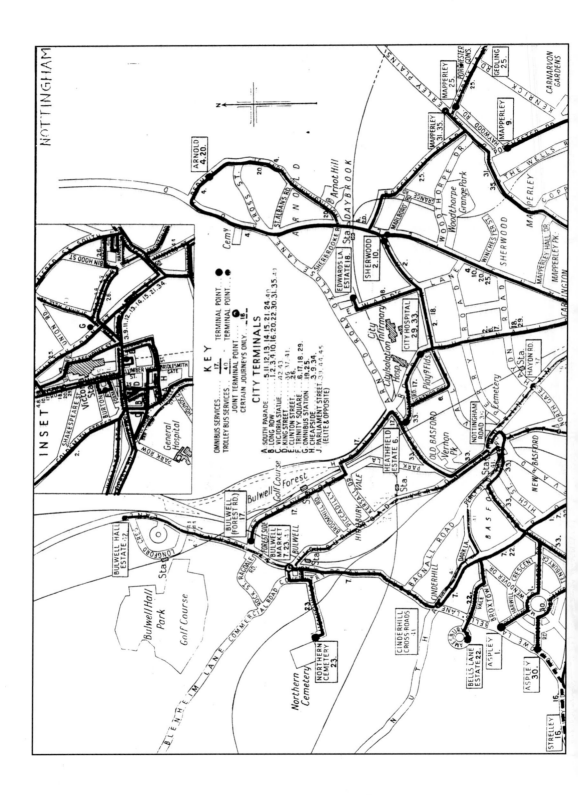

NOTTINGHAM

KEY

TERMINAL POINT
TERMINAL POINT
JOINT TERMINAL POINT
CERTAIN JOURNEYS ONLY.

OMNIBUS SERVICES.
TROLLEY BUS SERVICES.

CITY TERMINALS

A SOUTH PARADE. 5.11.12.13.14.15.21.24.40.
B LONG ROW. 1.2.3.9.10.16.20.22.30.31.35.41.
C VICTORIA STATUE. 42.43
D KING STREET. 36.37.41.
E CLINTON STREET. 26.
F TRINITY SQUARE. 6.17.18.29.
G OMNIBUS STATION. 19.25.
H CHEAPSIDE. 3.9.34.
J PARLIAMENT STREET. 33.44.45.
(ELITE & OPPOSITE)

INSET

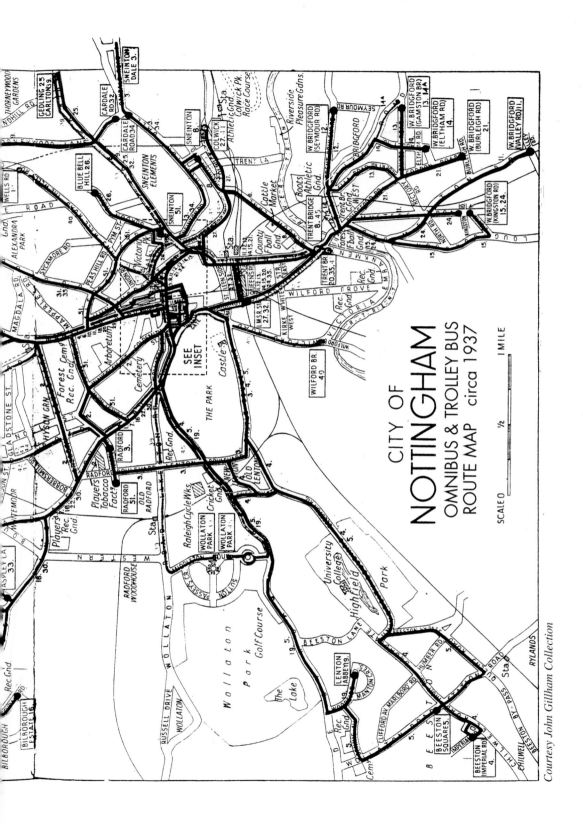

CITY OF NOTTINGHAM
OMNIBUS & TROLLEY BUS
ROUTE MAP circa 1937

SCALE 0   ½   1 MILE

Courtesy John Gillham Collection

69

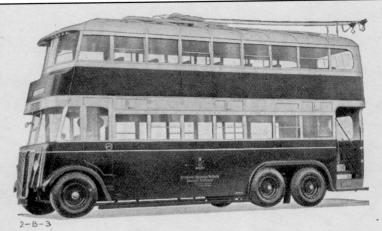

2-B-3

For every Requirement !

Whether your demands be for petrol, heavy oil or electric omnibuses, four-wheel or six-wheel, single or double-deck, you will find in the Karrier range, vehicles which for dignity of appearance, ease of maintenance, dependable performance, low operating cost and long life, are unexcelled.

26 to 68 seaters.

Literature on request to

KARRIER MOTORS LTD., HUDDERSFIELD.

DECIDE ON "KARRIER" Commercial Motor Vehicles TRADE MARK

THERE WILL BE NO REGRETS

One sunless Autumn 1938 day as Geoffrey Atkins was taking a stroll, camera at the ready as always, he came across the scene so graphically illustrated on this and the next page. Nottingham's AEC Regent No. **210** (**CTO 384**), which had entered service in October 1936 and was thus almost new in these pictures, had come to grief in Mansfield Road at The Forest while working service 10 to Sherwood. The Metro-Cammell metal-framed bodywork has obviously taken the shock of falling onto its side extremely well: a testament to its rigidity and constructional strength. Perhaps the most remarkable aspect is that there appear to be no broken windows, borne out by the lack of broken glass on the road. In the general view on the next page Nottingham's AEC tower wagon *(see page 49)* can be seen, as, in the distance, can 1931 Brush-bodied Ransomes trolleybus No. **42** (**TV 4480**). *(All: GHFA)*